A HIGH PLACE WITH A BEAUTIFUL VIEW

Blue Mound State Park

Albert M. Swain

LITTLE CREEK PRESS®
AND BOOK DESIGN
MINERAL POINT, WISCONSIN

Copyright © 2019 Albert M. Swain

Little Creek Press®
A Division of Kristin Mitchell Design, Inc.
5341 Sunny Ridge Road
Mineral Point, Wisconsin 53565

Book Design and Project Coordination:
Little Creek Press

First Printing
August 2021

All rights reserved

No part of this book may be used or reproduced
in any manner whatsoever without written
permission from the author.

Printed in the United States of America

To order books: www.littlecreekpress.com

ISBN-13: 978-1-955656-08-5

Table of Contents

Acknowledgments 6

Welcome to Blue Mounds State Park 7

Chapter One | Top of the Mound, Picnic Area and Towers 10

Chapter Two | Hiking from the Park Entrance into the Campground 21

Chapter Three | A Hike on the John Minix Trail 24

Chapter Four | A Hike into Pleasure Valley 31

About the Author 36

Appendix 37

To
My wife
Astrid J. Swain

Acknowledgments

This book would not have been possible without the support and encouragement of the Friends of Blue Mound State Park. The writing began as a result of a comment made to me by Park Manager Kevin Swenson at a Friends meeting. "When are you going to write a book about this park?" Because of my 13 years as park naturalist and park researcher, he felt that my accumulated knowledge of the park should be written down. My years at Blue Mound State Park would not have happened if Karl Heil had not hired me as park naturalist back in 2000. Thank you, Karl.

Many hours discussing book content regarding the inclusion of photos and written material with Diane Stojanovich were essential for keeping the writing on track. Andrea Quisling, daughter of Sverre Quisling who owned Pleasure Valley Ski Resort, provided many newspaper clippings about the resort. Karsten Berge provided valuable information regarding the location of the ski jump and the Pioneer Village in Pleasure Valley. The Blue Mound State Park office provided many historical photographs.

Most of all, I thank my wife, Astrid, for being my hiking partner for over 55 years. After all of the hikes she has accompanied me on in Blue Mound State Park over the years, she could play park naturalist in my absence. I also give her credit for some of my photos as she spots beautiful scenes and flowers that I miss because I am partially red-green colorblind.

Photo credit: Wisconsin Department of Natural Resources

Welcome to Blue Mound State Park

Why Blue Mound? Perhaps it should be called green mound because of the relatively dense cover of forest vegetation. It only appears blue when viewed from a distance. Blue Mound is not a very unique name, as any object that can be seen from a distance has a bluish appearance. Humidity in the air creates the blue color so that increases in distance from the mound, or increases in relative humidity enhances the color. I believe that the Native Americans, Ho-Chunk/Winnebago, had a better name for Blue Mound called Weehaukaja which translates as "a high place with a beautiful view." They also believed that the bluish haze on the mound (photo 2) was caused by the Great Spirit smoking his peace pipe. Because of the elevational relief, Blue Mound may rate mountain status as the climate can be different between the top of the mound and the village of Blue Mounds below. It is not unusual to have the top of the mound in the clouds while the air is clear in the village.

There are really two mounds—West Blue Mound (Blue Mound State Park) and East Blue Mound (Brigham County Park). The village below and immediately south of the mounds is called Blue Mounds with an "s". When the village was located about one-half mile west of its present location prior to 1881, its official name was West Blue Mound. However, it was usually called Pokerville by the locals as it was populated by miners who spent their evenings drinking and playing poker.

2. East side of West Blue Mound viewed from Forshaug Road located about four miles east. The top of the mound has a bluish appearance.

Because the railroad was completed in 1881 with its depot located east in the present village, most of the residents moved east as well. West Blue Mound, with an elevation of 1,716 feet, is about 225 feet higher than East Blue Mound. Blue Mound State Park is the highest point in the southern half of Wisconsin and is the seventh highest point in the state. The top of Blue Mound State Park is a prominent feature on the landscape as it can be viewed from 50 miles away.

The first recorded history of Blue Mounds begins with Jonathan Carver, an Englishman, who was exploring the Wisconsin River on October 9, 1776. He was probably staying in the Sauk City area as the mounds are visible from river level. He stated, "While staying here, I took view of some mountains that lie about 15 miles to the southward … I ascended one of these and had an extensive view of the country." Blue Mound State Park is a relatively young state park compared to

4. Park entrance sign from 1938–48 when the park was privately owned. Note that the elevation is actually 1,716 feet rather than 1,760 feet.

3. Entrance sign to Blue Mound State Park.

6. A large white oak greets visitors as they arrive at the top of the mound.

A High Place with a Beautiful View

many of Wisconsin's parks, but it has been used as a park longer than most others from the middle 1800s until 1959 when the state purchased it from private ownership. The private owners treated the property as a farm and as a park (photos 3, 4).

This book will introduce the park's unique geology, biology, and its long history as a park and farm by guiding you through four diverse hikes (photo 1). Because the park is known as the highest point in southern Wisconsin, the first hike emphasizes the top of the park. The second hike begins at the entrance station and circles through the campground. The third hike begins at the Friends Shelter and follows the popular John Minix Trail through a mixed hardwood forest and past sinkholes. The fourth hike also starts at the Friends Shelter and leads you down about 300 feet past maple forests and a prairie into Pleasure Valley where a ski resort once existed. For a detailed history of the township surrounding most of Blue Mound State Park, read *Weehaukaja* by John F. Helmenstine 1976–77.

The new office/visitor station.

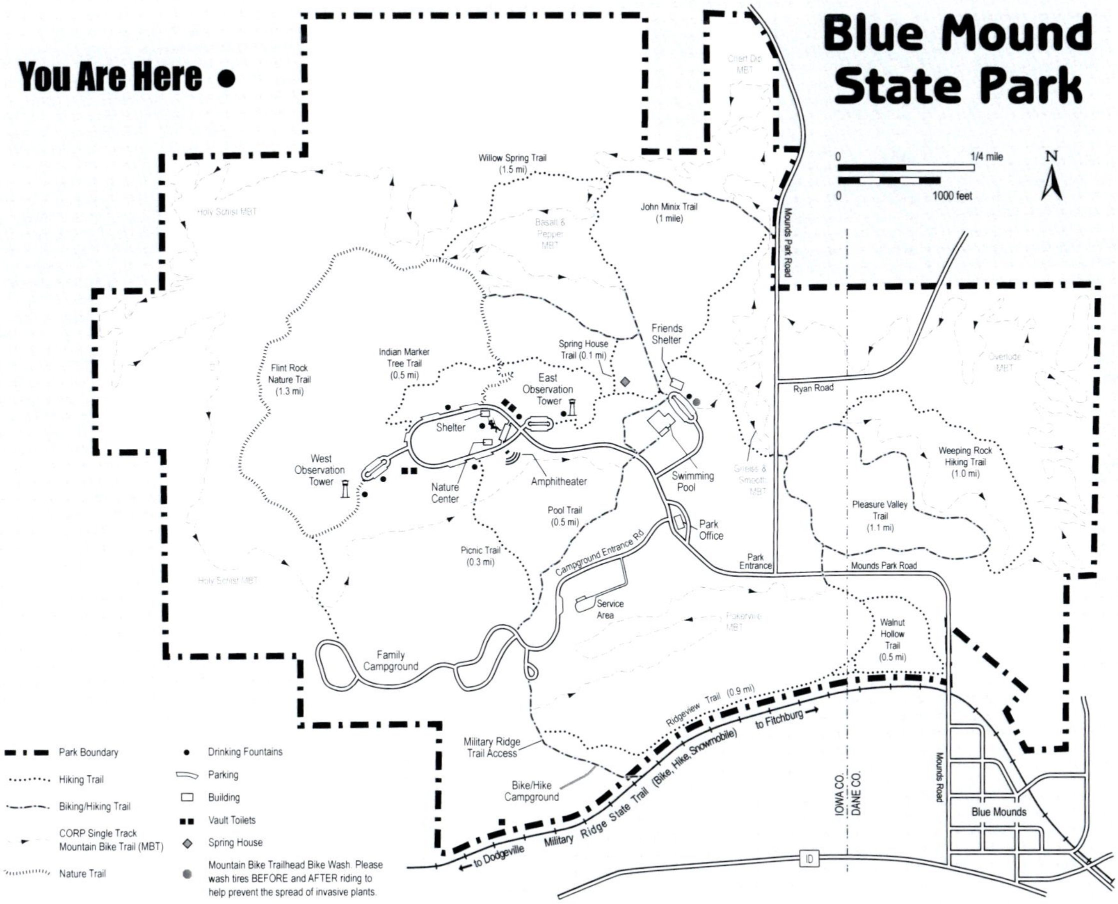

1.

Chapter One
TOP OF THE MOUND, PICNIC AREA, AND TOWERS

Welcome to Blue Mound State Park! After passing the park entrance sign, the office/entrance station or Public Entrance Visitor Service (PEVS), and arriving at the picnic area on top of the mound, you are now at the highest point in southern Wisconsin. First-time visitors to the park find the views from the top of the mound awe-inspiring. I have been surprised at how underused this jewel (photo 6) of a park has been by residents living within a 30-mile radius of Blue Mounds. It is not uncommon to find on one of my hikes a long-time resident visiting the park for the first time. This part of the park west of Mounds Park Road was owned privately from the mid-1800s until 1959 when it became a state park. Private properties east of that road were added to the park during the next two decades.

After arriving in the east parking lot, we will begin our hike by climbing the 40-foot east observation tower (photo 7). After the hikers catch their breath and have a chance to experience how high they are above the local landscape, I relate to them that they may be seeing 25 to 60 miles depending on their viewing direction (photos 8, 9). On clear

8. View to the northeast from the east tower.

7. East tower—40 feet high.

10a. Landmark locator.

9. A view to the northeast from the top of the mound in 1937.

11. Aerial view showing the top of the mound and farmland to the south.

days one can see the capitol in Madison (photo 10) about 25 miles east and the Baraboo Range about 25 miles north. A spotting device mounted on top of the tower helps locate distant objects (photo 10a). The forested landscape north of the mound contrasts with the agriculturally dominated view to the south of the mound. Because the topography on the north side of the mound is quite rugged with deep valleys and steep-sided hills, agriculture is limited to ridgetops and valley bottoms (photo 11). Brigham Park and the water towers in Mt. Horeb are visible to the east of the village of Blue Mounds. South of the park, note the unusual

10. View from the east tower showing the state capitol. The dome is in the top center of the photo.

locations of clumps of trees and shrubs in the middle of fields rather than along fence lines. They are growing out of rock piles (tailings) from surface lead mining operations less than 50 feet deep from the 1800s.

While on the tower, be on the lookout for large black birds soaring in the thermals next to the

Blue Mound State Park

mound. These are turkey vultures, and they use their excellent eyesight and sense of smell help to locate decomposing food (Robbins, Brunn and Zim. 1966).

My wife and I have always encouraged visitors to the park to see the scenic views from the towers and vistas on top of the mound (photo 12). It is truly surprising that many people have visited the park several times without experiencing the magnificent views from the top of the park. I met one individual who had camped with his family several times yet had only experienced the campground and the swimming pool. He was surprised to find out about the towers and fantastic views. As we hike west from the east tower, we pass by several large, open-grown white oaks (photos 12, 13) to a monument located at the edge of a large clearing that once represented the location of a radio station (WIBA) and tower. The monument honors four servicemen who died in a plane crash about 11:50 p.m. on Saturday, November 25, 1944, about 200 feet below the top of the mound and north of the monument. Three crew members and one army private were flying from Chicago to Minneapolis in a C-47 (a military cargo plane) and encountered icing conditions near LaCrosse, Wisconsin (photos 14, 15) (Air Force Historical Research Agency. 1944). They

12. Open-grown white oak with the east tower showing along the right edge of the trunk.

13. White oak ecology.

14. Memorial monument for four men killed in the 1944 plane crash.

15. Memorial Day service. On the left, a nephew of the copilot observes the ceremony.

continued to have icing issues and were told that they could fly safely at 1,500 feet southeast back to Lone Rock, Wisconsin, which had a runway that could accommodate military aircraft during World War II and was located about 20 miles northwest of Blue Mound. They either didn't hear the radio message or ignored it and continued past Lone Rock toward Chicago and crashed into the northeast corner of Blue Mound at 1,500 feet (200 feet below the top of the mound). I suspect the young crew preferred flying back to Chicago rather than being stuck in Lone Rock for the weekend.

The crash site was not found until the following Monday when a search plane was sent out to locate the wreckage. A local farmer had heard the crash and saw fire but did not report the incident until talking with a neighbor on Monday. The pilot and radioman were thrown clear of the wreckage, and only the pilot was still alive when found by the rescue crew. The pilot was suffering from hypothermia and died in the military hospital at Truax Airport in Madison two days later. Doctors at the hospital said that the pilot and radioman would have survived if they had been found soon after the crash. A thunderstorm with freezing rain and snow contributed to the deaths of those two individuals.

The official crash report had determined that the incident was caused by human error. Meteorologists in Chicago warned the crew of marginal flying conditions. Because their licenses permitted them to fly in such weather, and they had flown many missions from India to China during World War II, they felt comfortable making this flight to Minneapolis. Also, they should have landed in Lone Rock. They would have missed the mound if they had not been two miles off course or another quarter mile farther off course. Unfortunately, Blue Mound is the highest point between Chicago and Minneapolis. It's my opinion that the pilot wanted to make this flight since his home town was Minneapolis and he would have liked to have visited family and possibly a girlfriend and to show the crew a good time about town. The crash site is marked by an information sign on the Willow Spring Trail next to four shagbark hickories (photos 16, 17). A few small artifacts from the crash were found with metal detectors between 2002 and 2010.

16. A C-47 crash site sign located on the Willow Springs Trail.

17. Shagbark hickory information sign.

A short distance west of the military monument is a second monument dedicated to John Minix who with his wife Matilda owned the park from 1933 to 1959 (photo 18, 19). He was killed in the park in 1947 on his 70th birthday when he was run over by a dump truck as he tried to jump on the side of it to inspect a load of gravel. His wife and two of her brothers continued to operate the park until 1959 when the state purchased it as a park. Matilda may have made more money if she had sold it to private developers, but fortunately, she always wanted the property to remain a park. I interviewed a nephew 40 years after the sale, and he was still complaining that she sold the park too cheaply. However, John Minix originally purchased the property at a sheriff's sale, so there should have been substantial profit. More about John and Matilda is discussed later.

From the Minix monument, we continue west along the north loop of a road that was once a half-mile long horse-racing track in the 1890s (photo 20). Special trains brought visitors from the Madison area to Blue Mounds on weekends to watch the races, picnic, play baseball, and enjoy the scenery. Large businesses in Madison often used the park for annual picnics. A copy of an 1897 photo showing a Fourth of July celebration on top of the mound included folks dressed in their finest—women in long dresses carrying parasols and men in suits and bowties (photos 21, 22). Large canvas tents, horses, carriages, and men playing baseball are seen on one or more of the photos. Copies of these photos are on display in the park's nature center located south of the large picnic shelter.

18. John Minix memorial.

19. Park brochure printed by the Minix family prior to 1959.

20. Aerial view to the north showing the park road on top of the mound that was a half-mile long horse-racing track in the 1890s.

21.

22. 1897 Fourth of July celebration. Note the baseball game, fancy attire, and carriages.

23. Nature Center. It's the only building remaining from the Minix ownership.

24. Picnic shelter. The swings were removed in 2017 for new playground equipment.

The nature center was once a concession stand built in the 1940s to provide refreshments during home talent baseball games (photo 23). The nature center now houses displays of photos, information on prairies and caves, and mounted birds. Three outside ledges with boarded up windows indicate where visitors were served. The building is constructed of local bedrock and was designed by a colleague of Frank Lloyd Wright and may account for the unusual roofline.

The baseball diamond here was also used occasionally by Mt. Horeb High School when their field was too wet for playing. The bedrock on top of the mound allows for quick drainage. I talked with a man from New Glarus who played on the Blue Mound diamond against Mt. Horeb in the early 1950s when the Mt. Horeb diamond was too wet. The New Glarus team members had been told to bring old clothes and a flashlight to the game as they were going caving in the park after the game.

Before the property became a state park, access to two caves was possible by climbing down 25-foot vertical shafts on rope ladders to the cave floors. One cave is about 150 feet long and the other is 50 feet. Access to the caves is now restricted because of safety issues. Currently, the shelter and the adjacent open field are used for picnics, games, meetings, and other family gatherings (photos 24, 25, 26, 26a). The shelter and the nearby vista can be reserved for family gatherings, meetings, and weddings (photo 25a).

25a. Main vista, often used for weddings and large family gatherings.

25. Shelter and playground in 1935.

26. New playground equipment installed in 2017.

26a. Sign recognizing those who donated the playground equipment.

Continuing west along the north side of the mound top you will pass several vistas to a sign for the Indian Marker Tree Trail (photo 27). Less than 100 yards down the trail, an old white oak stood with its lower trunk bent in such a way that it pointed to the spot where the sun rises on the first day of summer. The tree was at least 150 to 170 years old when it died in 2003. The age was determined by removing a small core slightly smaller than a pencil from near the base of the tree with an increment corer that screws into the tree. In the spring of 2016, the tree finally fell. Similar marker

INDIAN MARKER TREE

When this white oak was a young sapling, Native Americans bent the tree in place with leather straps or notched sticks so it would point toward a significant sight. This tree and most Wisconsin marker trees are white oaks and accurately point toward the location on the horizon where the sun rises on the first day of summer. Although the tree was thought to point toward a large spring on the east edge of the mound, it actually points about 25 degrees north of the spring.

This marker tree, now dead, was about 150 to 170 years old when it died in 2003. White oaks were probably used as marker trees as they bend easily without breaking and live a long time even when stressed.

27. Sign at the Indian Marker Tree.

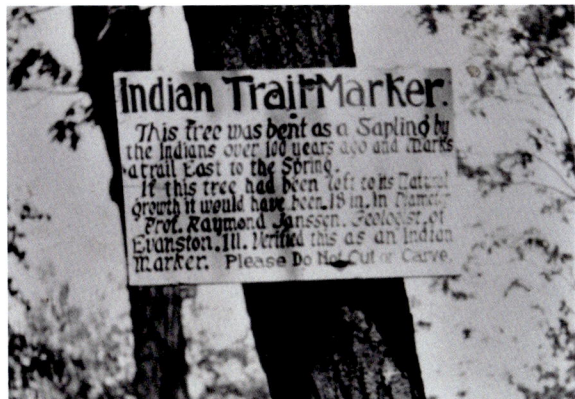

28. Indian Marker Tree sign from 1937.

trees have been found elsewhere in Wisconsin and adjacent states that also mark the sunrise location for the summer solstice. Prior to 2003, an information sign next to the tree stated that the tree pointed to a large spring at the east end of the mound (photo 28). Native Americans believed that drinking water from this spring would ensure that they would go to the happy hunting ground if killed in battle. However, the tree pointed about 30 degrees north of that location. I believe that the Native Americans could have done a better job pointing the tree to the spring if that had been their intention. White oaks tended to be the tree of choice for marker trees as they are quite flexible like saplings and can withstand considerable bending. Straps, ropes, or forked branches were probably used to hold the bent sapling in place. Because of the age of the tree, it's believed that the Ho-Chunk may have created the marker tree. About five different tribes are known to have occupied this area. The Iowans were the earliest, which gave rise to Iowa County and the state of Iowa. The latest group was the Winnebago/Ho-Chunk tribe who are still active in the area.

Besides seeing the marker tree, the remainder of the Marker Tree Trail is worth hiking as cliffs and variable forest vegetation make the trail unique. Instead of white oak and shagbark hickory, which dominate the south side of the mound, you will see

29. Interrupted ferns. Reproductive spores are produced in the dark areas in each leaf.

a mix of red oak, ash, sugar maple, aspen, paper birch, and only a few scattered white oaks and shagbark hickories. Another outstanding feature of the trail is the abundance of ferns, particularly the large interrupted fern (photo 29). The presence of blueberries, Canadian mayflowers, bush honeysuckle, and several other herbs and shrubs are reminiscent of forests found 100 to 200 miles farther north in Wisconsin (photos 30, 31, 32, 33, 34). Plant names used in this book follow those listed in the following references: Courtenay and Zimmerman, 1972, Petrides, 1958. The northern exposure of the slope along this trail creates a cooler and moist environment similar to locations farther north in the state. It is not unusual for plants growing on this side of the mound to flower two weeks later than the same plants on the south side. Most of the forest is relatively young—originating after about 1930. The presence of

32. Blueberries.

30. Canadian star flower.

33. Wild lily of the valley or Canadian Mayflower.

31. Bush honeysuckle.

36. Poison ivy in fall color.

Top: 34. Cliff fern.

Left: 35. Niagara dolomite or limestone—also called chert or flint rock.

38. View from the west tower with the city of Barneveld visible in left-center.

a few large open-grown trees with large lower dead or living branches on this and other trails suggests that the forest was much more open than at present.

Cliff ferns, mosses, and lichens decorate the cliffs along the trail. The cliffs and large boulders consist of a very hard rock called Niagara dolomite (also called flint rock or chert) that is about 400 million years old (photo 35). Much of the magnesium and calcium has been removed and replaced with silica, which makes the rock extremely hard and resistant to erosion, thus protecting the top of the mound. The rock is the same age and composition as that at Niagara Falls, hence the name Niagara (Dott and Attig. 2004). Native Americans and early settlers collected the rock for flint to start fires. Because the rock has extremely sharp edges when broken or worked, the Native Americans also used the rock for making arrowheads and other stone tools. Hikers using the Indian Marker Tree Trail should be aware of the presence of poison ivy and stay on the trail while hiking (photo 36).

37. View from the west tower. Platte Mound located near Platteville, Wisconsin, is visible in the distance.

Poison ivy is prevalent in the park, and the same warning should be considered on all park trails.

A short hike west of the Marker Tree Trail sign brings you to the west tower. Southwest from this location one can see 30 to 45 miles to Belmont Mound, Platte Mound with a large M on its west slope, and a third mound located near the Wisconsin/Illinois border (photos 37, 38). On a clear day, if you know where to look, the west bank of the Mississippi River is visible in Iowa over 60 miles west of the park. The Military Ridge Bicycle Trail is also visible between the park and Barneveld located four miles west of the park. Both towers make excellent platforms for viewing fireworks displays during Fourth of July celebrations. As many as six displays may be visible at one time. However, you will only hear the Mt. Horeb and Barneveld fireworks. Hiking east along the south loop of the summit road you will pass the amphitheater on the south side of the road (photo 39, see map for location). Prior to the construction of the Friends Shelter in 2013, most

39. Amphitheater.

park programs were presented here on weekends for park visitors. The programs were varied and included nature programs with talks, slideshows and videos, and a variety of musical events. It was always fun to watch how children and parents reacted during snake programs. It was the parents who were the most squeamish about touching snakes.

I once had a raccoon upstage me during a presentation about the park and its wildlife (photo 40). I had just finished showing a slide of a raccoon when a live raccoon waddled out of the woods from behind the stage and continued along the left side of the stage and across the front to the steps on the right side of the stage. Then it climbed the steps to the stage floor and walked slowly to the front edge of the stage and looked out at the

40. Raccoon visiting a campsite at dusk.

audience for a few seconds and then turned and left and disappeared into the woods. I lost the audience—they thought I had a trained raccoon. I should have said, "Rascal, be back next week at the same time." Several years later I presented the same program and mentioned the raccoon appearance. A man in the audience yelled out, "I was there." Raccoons are quite common in the park and are generally nocturnal. They are fun to observe but can be a nuisance to your food in the campground. They eat anything humans eat and are quite capable of opening food containers with toes that work like human fingers. Park visitors should not intentionally feed raccoons as it makes them incredibly bold and difficult to scare away from your dining area.

Before leaving the mound top (picnic area) one should note the number of hiking trails leading to other parts of the park (see park map) such as the campground (photo 41), swimming pool, or the Flint Rock Trail.

41. A typical campsite with fire ring and picnic table. The 78 campsites are relatively secluded and shaded. Electricity is provided at 17 reservable and 6 non-reservable sites.

Chapter Two
HIKING FROM THE PARK ENTRANCE INTO THE CAMPGROUND

The second hike is a two-mile loop that starts at the entrance station (PEVS) and continues to the west end of the campground and back. This is an interesting area even if you are not camping. The loop may be traversed on foot, bicycle, or by car. Generally, hiking in this area is done without the aid of a park naturalist as a leader. For most visitors, this loop is initially done by car as they survey the campground for a potential campsite that fits their needs—seclusion, shade, electricity, levelness, and closeness to water and toilets. The last thing they are concerned about is what trees,

42. Shower building with flush toilets. Three sets of pit toilets are available in other areas of the campground.

shrubs, and other flowering plants are present. Only once the campers are settled in at a site do they begin to explore the campground. Other park visitors who are not camping often hike through the campground as several trails pass through or originate there.

The campground is located along the south slope of the mound and is distinctly warmer and drier than the north and east sides of the mound (photo 41).

The early land office survey records from the 1800s showed that this side of the mound was a savanna with scattered trees and prairie. The campground is currently dominated by a forest of white oaks and shagbark hickories (see photos below). Prairie plants are nearly nonexistent. Hickory nuts are visitor favorites as they taste nearly identical to pecans. Pecans are actually hickory trees that grow in states south of Wisconsin. Park visitors

Left: white oak. Right: Shagbark hickory.

may collect nuts and fruits in the park for their own use. Removing whole plants and flowers is restricted by law in Wisconsin state parks. A single sheet nature guide that introduces park visitors to their green neighbors is generally available at the shower building in the campground (photo 42). Although the campground is open for camping year-round, the campground roads are not plowed in the winter as they serve as cross-country ski trails.

Directly east and adjacent to the campground is the service area, which was the location of the original farm buildings prior to 1959. At that

43. Minix farmhouse and toll gate.

43b. Sheep grazing adjacent to the springhouse. The area below the springhouse was developed as a swimming pool by 1937. The springhouse became the concession stand for the pool.

43a. Swain Prairie.

time, the original entrance road went directly west, somewhat short of the current park office, to the farm. There was a gate next to the farmhouse where fees were collected. (photo 43) Farming was basically subsistence and supplemented with income from visitor fees. Cows, sheep, horses, and pigs were raised during the period of private ownership prior to 1959. The main part of the park that is in Iowa County has never been plowed because of rocky shallow soils. Several areas were cleared for hay crops or pasture. The top of the mound was cut for hay. An area along the trail from campsite 8 south to the Military Ridge Bike Trail may have been used as pasture or a hay crop. This remnant prairie has been restored by removing invaded trees and shrubs followed by prescribed burns (photo 43a, map (C)). Between this prairie and the Military Ridge Bike Trail (photo 43c) is a bike campground (photo 43d) with 12 campsites, water and toilets. Photos from the 1930s show sheep grazing in the area that is now the swimming pool and shelter parking lot. (photo 43b)

As you travel through the campground, you will see a handicap accessible cabin, tent pads, and six electrical sites in the far west end of the campground that were paid for by the Friends of Blue Mound State Park. (photo 44) Other Friends contributions include the Friends Shelter, snow grooming equipment, salary for a part-time park naturalist, and some financial support for the new splash pad/pool. The Friends organization has been important in supporting the park since the 1990s and has sponsored trail runs and bike rides for many of those years.

43d. Entrance to the bicycle campground.

44. Handicap accessible cabin located near the shower building.

43c. A maple forest along the Military Ridge Bike Trail located near the trail to the bicycle campground.

Chapter Three
A HIKE ON THE JOHN MINIX TRAIL

The third hike includes the John Minix trail and the trailhead area next to the Friends Shelter and swimming pool. The Minix Trail is a one-mile loop starting at the Friends Shelter (see map (D), photo 45). The area next to the Friends Shelter

45. Friends Shelter completed in 2013.

is also the trailhead for several hiking, biking, and cross-country ski trails. The pool and splash pad along the west edge of the parking lot were new in 2015 and replaced a larger pool that had a diving area and a children's wading pool that served the Blue Mounds area from about 1970 to 2014. (photo 46) An earlier pool existed from

46. Current splash pad and pool.

47. Construction of the 1971 pool.

48. The completed 1971 pool.

1937 to 1959 when the park was owned by John Minix. (pool photos 47, 48) Because the Minix pool existed before the property became a state park, a new pool was grandfathered in about ten years later, apparently with some pressure from residents. The original pool, nearly as large as the pool constructed in 1971, was built of concrete with limestone steps leading into the swimming area. A concrete wall divided the pool into two halves—one half for swimming and one half for fishing. Minix stocked trout in the fishing half (photo 49). The pool's water source came from

49. The Minix pool completed in 1937. Note the springhouse on the left and the bath house on the right. The fishing portion of the pool is on the left.

a springhouse located just a few yards uphill from the pool. The water was an invigorating 50 degrees when it entered the pool and was warmed by sunshine. Personal friends who used the pool in the 1950s said that they just about popped out of the pool when they jumped into the cold water. I interviewed a man who worked for the Minix family in the '50s, and he was in charge of putting chlorine bleach water into the pool to disinfect it. Kids would yell at him to refrain from putting in the bleach water as they claimed their eyes were burning and their swimming suits were dissolving. He put it in anyway. Attractive willow trees surrounded the pool, and only one or two were still standing by 2015. Now abundant sapling willows fill in the area where the pool once existed.

The springhouse doubled as a concession stand as well. The concrete floor still exists, and the springs are still active. Geology controls the location of the springs as springs are common around the park at the elevation of the springhouse. This is where the Niagara dolomite, which makes up the upper 85–100 feet of the mound, meets Maquoketa shale just above the pool (Dott and Attig. 2004). Shale is mud that has become rock. Because the dolomite has many faults, water passes through easily until it reaches the shale which lacks faults and acts like a plastic sheet and forces the water out horizontally as springs. The Minix pool was located about 100 yards north of the existing pool and was a popular swimming location for people living within a 20-mile radius of Blue Mounds as no other constructed outdoor pools existed in the area at that time. Blue Mound State Park was and still is the only state park with a swimming pool, although many parks do have beaches along rivers or lakes.

The Minix Trail is a very popular, easy one-mile looped hiking and skiing trail. Naturalist-led hikes are also popular on this trail as the forest vegetation and geology allow for a variety of different titled hikes including food, medicine, and poison in the woods; southern Wisconsin forest trees and shrubs; and sinkholes and caves. It is also a self-guided trail with trail information signs that describe common forest trees and understory herbs. (photos 50, 51, 52) This trail is located along the north and east side of the mound and has a high diversity of plants like that along the

> **JOHN MINIX TRAIL**
>
> This one-mile trail starts in an area that was once an open meadow of about 30 acres prior to 1959 when the park was sold to the state by the Minix family who had owned the property since 1933. The first 800 to 900 feet of the trail in either direction passes through dense shrubs, grasses, sedges and a few small trees which have invaded the meadow since 1959. The hardwood species of red oak, white oak, shagbark hickory, basswood, ash and maple dominate the forest along the remainder of the trail.
>
> This trail might be called the sink-hole trail because there are at least seven sink holes located along the north section of the trail. One large sink hole is marked by an information sign.
>
> Up the hill or west of this sign, less than 100 yards, another pool once served as a popular swimming hole for local residents from 1937 to 1959. The remains of the spring house which doubled as a concession stand and water source for the pool still exists west of the old pool site. The pool was in two parts, one half for swimming and one half for fishing. Willows once surrounded the pool and a few large individuals are still present.
>
> As you hike, be vigilant for poison ivy which is common along this and many other trails in the park. In the photo below, note the three leaflets, two which are close together and one that is on a longer stalk. The leaflet margins may be nearly smooth or with a few large teeth. The leaves may be shiny in early spring and dull looking later. The plant can be a small shrub, one-half to three feet tall, or even a vine. All parts of the plant have an oil that causes an allergic reaction when in contact with the skin. Note that pets are not affected by poison ivy but can carry the oil on their fur and transfer it to you. For that reason, keep all pets restrained and on the trails.
>
>
>
> Sign provided by Friends BMSP   Photo by A. Swain

50. The John Minix Trail information sign.

RED OAK
(Quercus rubra)

Red oak trees are common throughout most of Wisconsin particularly on relatively moist sites such as the north and east sides of the mound. It gets its name from the reddish color of the wood. This color and its distinctive grain pattern make the wood a popular choice for flooring and furniture.

The leaves have bristle-tipped lobes unlike white oak which has rounded tips. The bark is nearly black with flat-topped ridges.

Red oak acorns take two years to mature (white oak acorns take one year) and are very bitter and unfit for human consumption.

Red oaks sprout readily when the tops of young trees are damaged by fire or eaten by deer or domesticated animals. Note the multiple trunks at this location. Oak forests often have an abundant ground cover of herbs and shrubs as sunlight easily reaches the ground surface because the branching pattern does not produce a continuous layer of leaf cover that is typical of maple trees.

The photos below show three common plants in this area: left is jack-in-the- pulpit; center is wild geranium; and right is woodbine or Virginia creeper which also grows about one foot tall on the ground surface.

Sign provided by Friends BMSP   Photos by A. Swain

51. Red oak ecology and trail information along the Minix Trail.

WHITE ASH
(Fraxinus americana)

In Blue Mound State Park white ash is often found mixed with sugar maple, red oak, basswood and white oak. Ash trees are well known for their wood which is hard but can also withstand shock. For those reasons ash is used for baseball bats and hammer handles.

The photos show only one leaf which usually has seven leaflets (sometimes 5 or 9). The underside of the leaflets are light green in color which gives the tree its name.

The bark of older trees has ridges that are interconnected to form diamond-like patterns. The fruits shown in the lower photo have wings for wind dispersal.

White ash is common in upland sites while two other common ashes, the red and green ashes, usually grow in lowland settings. All three of these species look much alike and are sometimes difficult to distinguish.

In recent years a fungus/mold, which is carried by an insect called the emerald ash borer, has become a serious problem in many states east of Wisconsin. Large populations of ash have been destroyed in forests and along city streets. As of 2012, the disease has not been found in Blue Mound State Park. Because ash, oak and hickory make excellent firewood, only local sources of wood for campfires should be used. The borer and fungus are found under the bark and can be easily transported.

Sign provided by Friends BMSP   Photos by A. Swain

52. Ash ecology.

Indian Marker Tree Trail. If one knew the plants well, I believe one could successfully survive a summer in the park without the need for store-bought groceries. Becoming familiar with the flora in areas where you hike has other benefits other than food. I find that when I am hiking in a familiar area, the trees and other flowers are like seeing old friends, especially when I can put a name on them. This works with human encounters as well. Have you ever been in a large store with lots of shoppers and you are oblivious to the other shoppers until you see someone you know? After being introduced to a person or a tree, you start seeing them everywhere. Taking advantage of hikes with a naturalist helps you get introduced to your green friends. This is one of the reasons that naturalists enjoy being naturalists.

When starting a hike on the Minix Trail, the first several hundred yards along both the east and west portions of the trail are dominated by shrubs and wetland species. This area was a meadow prior to 1959 and was grazed or cut for fodder. This relatively flat and poorly drained region is related to the impermeable layer of shale located here. Before proceeding far on this trail, poison ivy and wild parsnip (see photos 36, 53), two untouchables, are introduced to visitors on naturalist-led hikes (Czarapata. 2005). Poison ivy has three leaflets per leaf, and all parts of the plant have an oil on the surface to which 90% of all humans are allergic. It appears that only humans

36. Poison Ivy.

A High Place with a Beautiful View

are allergic to the oil. The first time you touch poison ivy, there is no reaction because you have no antibodies against the oil. During the second and successive occurrences, it's a different story. The reaction may be only a rash where you were touched, or in rare cases, the whole body reacts, and emergency care is required. When a young child runs off a campsite into the woods loaded with poison ivy with the parents in hot pursuit, the mom and dad are the only ones who may get a poison ivy reaction as the child has never been exposed to poison ivy.

A grandfather on one of our hikes wondered why his grandson was getting rashes from poison ivy when he was not spending any time in the woods. I asked if the boy had a dog. He said yes and said that the dog was allowed to run free in the woods adjacent to his home. Dogs and all other animals are not allergic to poison ivy but can carry the oil on their hair and skin and transfer it to humans. For that reason, keep pets on a leash when camping and hiking. Become familiar with the plant as many other plants with three leaflets such as strawberries and raspberries have good things to offer.

The rashes or burns resulting from contact with wild parsnip are not allergic reactions. When the juice from the plant gets on the skin in the presence of sunlight, severe burns similar to sunburns can result. The scarring can last weeks to over a year. Casual touching of the plant is not a problem unless a leaf or stem is broken to release fluid on the skin. Wearing protective clothing is essential when dealing with this plant.

One of the deadliest plants in Wisconsin grows along the Minix Trail in somewhat damp areas. It's called poison hemlock. Because the flower on this plant looks like the flowers of Queen Anne's Lace (also called wild carrot), people have died when they mistakenly collected poison hemlock roots to eat instead of the wild carrot (photos 54,

54. Queen Anne's lace or wild carrot.

53. Wild parsnip.

55. Poison hemlock. Queen Anne's lace has much finer divided leaves than poison hemlock.

55). Some plants are poisonous but can still be used for food. Mayapple plants are poisonous to eat, but the ripe fruits are edible. (photos 56, 57) Jack-in-the-pulpit underground stems are edible if dried or cooked. There is a chemical in the fresh parts that can cause the lining in your mouth and throat to swell, and you can choke to death.

56. Mayapple flower. The blossom is beneath two umbrella shaped leaves.

57. Mayapple fruit.

58. Poplar or quaking/trembling aspen branch and leaves.

58a. Willow branch and leaves.

59. Impatiens/touch-me-not/jewelweed.

Medicine in the woods includes aspirin in the small branches of aspen (also called poplar) and willows. (photos 58, 58a) The fluid in Impatiens (touch-me-not or jewelweed—see photo 59) has antihistamines in the stem that relieve the itch from mosquito bites, stinging nettle, and poison ivy. It even worked to relieve the pain from a bee sting a young girl experienced during one of my hikes on the Minix Trail. Interesting comments were heard from hikers who were checking out why the pretty blue spiderwort plants are called spiderworts. (photo 60) The gel in a broken leaf

60. Spiderwort.

leaves a fine thread as you pull your finger away from the surface of the leaf and resembles a thread from a spiderweb. Unaware that I could hear them, a couple standing near me said that the gel felt like K-Y jelly.™ It appears that wild plants provide for most human wants. Some plants provide multiple uses for humans such as the basswood tree. (photo 61) In spring, the expanding buds taste like fresh green peas when eaten raw. The basswood flowers

61. Basswood.

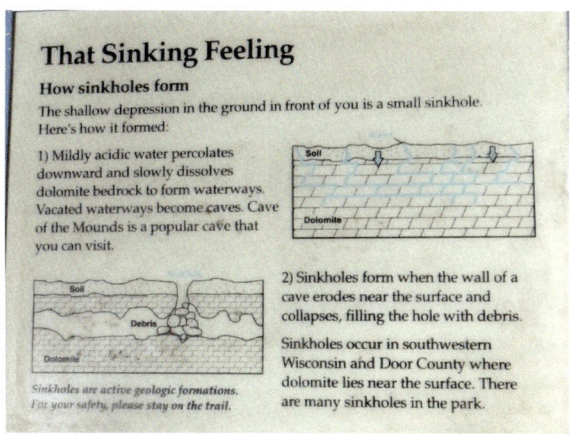
62. Sinkhole information sign.

63. Sinkhole.

82. Maple forest along the Weeping Rock Trail in Pleasure Valley.

and fruits make excellent tea. The inner bark has long threads that were used by Native Americans for making rope and thread. Native Americans and early settlers used the thorns from Hawthorn trees as needles. The relatively soft, white wood from basswoods is used for carvings.

Along the northern part of the Minix Trail loop, at least six sinkholes are visible near the trail or a few steps into the forest. (photos 62, 63) Sinkholes are collapsed cave roofs found in limestone bedrock. At this point along the trail, you are below the shale found at the trailhead. This limestone, called Galena dolomite, is the same as that at Cave of the Mounds located less than two miles east of the park. An information sign marks a sinkhole located near the northeast corner of the trail.

Along the eastern portion of the Minix Trail loop is a maple forest that borders the trail on the east side, while the west side is an oak forest. The difference between the two sides is quite striking.

Blue Mound State Park

SUGAR MAPLE
(Acer saccharum)

Sugar maple, a common forest tree here in Wisconsin and much of the northeastern United States, is known for maple syrup, sugar and wood for furniture. In the park, sugar maple is located in the cooler and more moist areas on the north and east slopes of the mound such as this location in front of you.

Sugar maple is very shade tolerant and the dense canopy of leaves produces extreme shade on the forest floor to the point where few other plants can grow with a few exceptions of ephemerals that bloom before the leaves appear on the trees. Ephemerals complete their entire life cycle in one or two months. Two examples are shown below: left is fawn or trout lily and right is toothwort. Both form large patches of green and white in April and May and completely disappear in early June. The forest floor is nearly bare during most of the year around the area in front of this sign. However, behind you the forest floor has an abundant cover of herbs, shrubs and tree seedlings because the canopy of the oak forest here allows light to reach the ground.

Around the second week of October, these maple leaves turn yellow or gold here as well as in the far east end of the park (Pleasure Valley).

Sign proveded by Friends BMSP   Photos by A. Swain

64. Sugar maple ecology and two common spring ephemerals.

65. Downy woodpecker.

The maple forest is exceptionally beautiful in the early spring with a display of spring ephemerals (plants with a short life cycle) and again in October when the maples turn yellow to gold. (photo 64, 82) The ephemerals often bloom and start producing fruit before the leaves appear on the trees. Very shortly the same plants turn yellow and completely disappear before the middle of June. After June the ground is bare except for maple seedlings. The west side oak forest is much more open with abundant sunlight reaching the forest floor that accounts for the variety of shrubs, tree seedlings, and herbs. The marked difference between the two sides of the trail probably resulted from different management as the two areas had different ownership prior to early 1970's.

During a slow walk on the Minix Trail you may spot evidence of past grazing. Look for pieces of wire protruding out of tree trunks, rolls of wire lying just off the trail, the presence of shrubs with thorns, and trees with multiple stems. Shrubs such as prickly ash expand in the area when grazing animals remove its competition by leaving thorny plants alone. As seedlings, the trees with multiple stems had their tops removed by grazing and sprouted back from the seedling base with multiple shoots as the original leader was absent.

On quiet early morning hikes, the Minix Trail is especially good for listening to bird calls and pecking sounds (photo 65). Learning to recognize bird calls is essential as most birds will not be visible. If you are quiet during the hike, you may see a few deer. Even on days when there is only a trace of a breeze, you may hear the rattling sound of aspen leaves. Quaking or trembling Aspen have leaves with flat petioles (stalks) which provide little support to the leaf compared to leaves on oak trees. Quaking/trembling probably should precede aspen as they are two different common names of aspen.

Chapter Four
A HIKE INTO PLEASURE VALLEY

Pleasure Valley is one of the lesser-known parts of the park because it is relatively remote from the main part of the park. Getting into the valley and back is about a two-and-a-half-mile hike with a total elevation change of about 200 feet. (photo 66) The hike involves the relatively easy Pleasure Valley Trail and the more difficult Weeping Rock Trail which goes down into the valley itself. After leaving the Friends Shelter you will pass through a maple forest before crossing Mounds Park Road to a fork in the trail. (see map) This part of the park east of Mounds Park Road is mainly in Dane County. Staying right at the fork takes you through assorted conifers (mostly white pine and Norway spruce (photo 67)) to the

67. Norway spruce (left) and white pine (right). Spruce needles are arranged singly along the branch, while white pine needles are in bundles of five.

west and south sides of the park prairie. As you enter the prairie, you can't help but appreciate the view to the east. The forest at the east end of the prairie forms the west edge of Pleasure Valley. The prairie was once a cornfield or other crops prior to becoming part of the state park. Farm buildings once stood immediately south of where you are standing (photo 68). This prairie is considered a

66. Pleasure Valley Trail sign.

68. The Wayne Mahoney farm was purchased by the park in 1972. Top of the photo is west. The farm is now a restored prairie. The farmhouse was moved into the Village of Blue Mounds.

Blue Mound State Park

69. Big bluestem grass.

69a. Indian grass.

70. *Liatris*/blazing star with an eastern tiger swallowtail butterfly.

72. Purple coneflower/ Echinacea.

73. Black-eyed Susan.

74. Prairie coneflowers.

71. Compass plant flowers. The stem is over seven feet tall.

tall grass prairie with big bluestem and Indian grass along with typical prairie flowers such as *Liatris* (blazing star), compass plant, prairie dock, black-eyed Susan, prairie coneflower, and assorted sunflowers. (see photos 69, 69a, 70, 71, 72, 73, 74) The prairie is burned at regular intervals to prevent shrubs and trees from encroaching. Fire does not hurt the prairie plants as they are perennials with underground stems that sprout back after a fire. After the prairie vegetation has been burned off, hundreds of anthills standing 4–10 inches high will be visible. (see photo 75)

75. The prairie after a burn.

Across the road from the south border of the prairie is a grass dominated slope surrounded by the Walnut Hollow Trail (map (E)). This area was part of the Pleasure Valley Ski Resort that is discussed in the following paragraphs (photos 76 and 76a (McCue. 2018)).

76. Part of the Pleasure Valley brochure describing the Crater Theater.

76a. The Crater Theater.

77. Weeping Rock Trail sign near the southeast corner of the prairie (junction of Weeping Rock and Overlode trails).

At the southeast corner of the prairie, you follow the Weeping Rock Trail into Pleasure Valley. (photo 77) Pleasure Valley was the name of a downhill ski resort that operated in the 1940s and 1950s with multiple ski slopes, two toboggan runs, an ice skating pond, two rope tows, a ski jump that held international competitions, and a Frontier Village (photos 78, 78a(D), 79, 80, 81). There was a tendency for the better skiers to over jump the slope and land on a flat surface (Berge, personal communication). Spectators at the ski jump often parked their cars in the valley bottom, and Berge's father made extra money with his tractor by pulling cars back up the steep slope to the highway. Berge said that Native Americans from the Wisconsin Dells area often stayed in some the of Frontier Village buildings during the summer. A ski lodge was located along the south

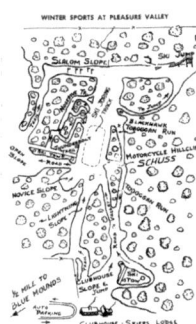

78. The inside page of the Pleasure Valley Resort brochure. The top of the map is north. The resort was owned and operated by Sverre Quisling (a surgeon in Madison, Wisconsin).

78a. This photo is a 1968 aerial view of the Pleasure Valley section of Blue Mound State Park. The top of the photo is east. (A) is Mounds Road to the right into Blue Mounds. (B) marks the entrance into Blue Mound State Park. (C) locates the buildings of the Pleasure Valley Resort. (D) was the location of the ski jump. (E) is a pond, and the short clear area east of the pond is the location of the Pioneer village. (F) is Ryan Road. The open area east of the curve in the road provided parking for activities in the valley. Cars could drive into the valley bottom from the open area and from the resort buildings. (G) marks the Mounds Park Road. The open area east of (G) is the Mahoney farm.

boundary of the resort about 0.2 miles east of the 90-degree bend in Mounds View Road that leads to the park entrance (photos 78b(C), 79). After the park closed, the lodge stayed open for a while as a bar/restaurant that catered to a younger crowd. Today only a concrete slab exists where the lodge once stood. Maples dominate the valley slopes. When these trees turn yellow in the fall, a walk down into the valley is an awesome experience. (photo 82) Pleasure Valley is the quietest and the coolest part of the entire park. Many park visitors on my guided hikes have told me that Pleasure Valley has become their favorite hiking area in all seasons. Several miles of mountain bike trails also wind through the hills in the valley. They also make spectacular hiking trails when the trees are leafless and the rugged topography is exposed. There are about 15 miles of mountain bike trails in the park largely constructed by WORBA (Wisconsin Off-Road Bicycle Association). (photos 83, 84) The trails in Pleasure Valley are among the

79. Pleasure Valley Resort. Top of the photo is east.

80. Frontier Village.

most scenic in the park. Following Weeping Rock Trail into a glen at about its lowest point, you will see a beautiful moss covered cliff with about six seepages leaking down the cliff into a rock-strewn stream. (photos 85, 86) After passing the cliff, the trail is all uphill (unfortunately) back to the Pleasure Valley Trail and finally the parking lot at the Friends Shelter. My advice is to take it slowly as there is more scenery to absorb, plank bridges to cross, clear-water pools with water striders, spring or fall color, and the exquisite quiet.

83. Snowshoeing in Pleasure Valley.

84. Mountain biking trail in Pleasure Valley.

81. Ski jump. This picture was on the front cover of the Pleasure Valley brochure.

85. Moss covered cliff with two stripes created by water leaking from the cliff face.

86. Water dripping from moss attached to the cliff face.

ABOUT THE AUTHOR
Albert M. Swain • December 1, 1940 – May 15, 2019

Albert M. Swain had a background in plant ecology and paleoecology from the University of Wisconsin-Madison and University of Minnesota-Minneapolis/St. Paul. One of Al's greatest passions was his service and contributions to Blue Mound State Park. He served as volunteer park naturalist for 13 years starting in 2000, a summer campground host, and was an active member of The Friends of Blue Mound State Park. In addition, he helped develop and grow an interpretive hiking program as well as conducting research projects pertaining to the history of the Blue Mound area, and the authoring of this book. In 2015, the 'Swain Prairie' was established at Blue Mound State Park in recognition of his efforts on this prairie restoration. Earlier experience involved research in forest and fire history in the Boundary Waters Canoe Area Wilderness in northern Minnesota and the Apostle Islands National Lakeshore in northern Wisconsin. For 13 years he worked at the Center for Climatic Research at the University of Wisconsin-Madison. His studies emphasized reconstructing past environments and climate back in time 1,000 to 16,000 years using pollen and charcoal analysis from cores of mud extracted from lakes in states from Washington to Maine. His teaching experience includes four years of high school biology and one semester of plant taxonomy at the University of Wisconsin-Platteville. The National Park Service honored him with a Special Service award in 1987 in recognition of his research and volunteerism. Until his untimely passing in May 2019, Al and his wife, Astrid, led senior hikes for the Senior Center in Verona, Wisconsin.

Al and Astrid Swain in Swain Prairie.

APPENDIX

References

Air Force Historical Research Agency. 1944. Plane crash at Blue Mounds, Wisconsin. Maxwell AFB, AL.

Berge, Karsten. 2018. Personal communication. Blue Mounds, Wisconsin. Karsten has lived nearly all of his life along Ryan Road adjacent to the northeast edge of Blue Mound State Park.

Courtenay, B. and J. H. Zimmerman. 1972. Wildflowers and Weeds. N.Y.; Van Nostrand and Reinhold. This is an excellent book about Wisconsin plants.

Czarapata, E. J. 2005. Invasive Plants of the Upper Midwest. Madison; University of Wisconsin Press.

Dott, R. H., Jr. and J. W. Attig. 2004. Roadside Geology of Wisconsin. Missoula, Montana; Mountain Press. This is a very easy to read and informative text about Wisconsin Geology.

Helmenstine, J. F. 1976. Weehaukaja—A History of the village of Barneveld and the Town of Brigham. Printed locally. The publication has two volumes. Volume One includes early history of what is now Blue Mound State Park that is in Iowa County. The large prairie and Pleasure Valley are in Dane County.

McCue, Andrea. 2017. Andrea, daughter of Sverre Quisling who owned Pleasure Valley Ski Resort, provided many newspaper clippings and park brochures regarding Pleasure Valley.

Petrides, G. A. 1958. A Field Guide to Trees and Shrubs. Boston; Houghton Mifflin.

Robbins, C. S., B. Bruun and H. S. Zim. 1966. Birds of North America. New York; Golden Press. The book is a standard for identifying North American birds.

Photo Credits

The majority of the photos were taken by the author. Photos 4, 9, 19, 21, 25, 28, 43, 43b, 47, 48, 49, 79, and 80 were from the photo and slide files at Blue Mound State Park. Photos 76a and 81 are from the Mt. Horeb Historical Society. Gail Van Haren provided photo 68.

TRAILS IN BLUE MOUNDS STATE PARK—summarized from the Blue Mound State Park Visitor Paper.

Hiking Trails (see map on page 9)
There are about ten miles of park hiking trails that also double as cross-country ski trails during the winter months. These include the Flint Rock Nature Trail, John Minix trail, Pleasure Valley Trail, Ridgeview Trail, Walnut Hollow Trail, and Willow Springs Trail. They are all relatively easy hiking trails except Ridgeview and Walnut Hollow trails, which are moderately difficult. Two other hiking only trails include the Indian Marker (moderate hiking difficulty) and Weeping Rock (difficult hiking).

Cross-country Skiing (see map on page 9)
About nine miles of groomed and tracked trails exist in the park. The trailhead for most of the trails begins at the swimming pool parking lot. The ski trails, bike trails, and hiking trails are all in wooded terrain except the Pleasure Valley Trail which starts in a maple forest and then follows the edge of an open prairie. The John Minix (1 mile) and the Willow Springs (2 miles) trails

are the easiest ski trails (yellow to green, level to moderately hilly). The Flint Rock (4 miles) is slightly more difficult (red) with moderate to steep hills. The Ridge View and Walnut Hollow trails (blue, 5 miles) have several steep downhill runs that can be challenging and not recommended for beginning skiers. The Pleasure Valley Trail (2 miles, orange) is only moderately hilly except for one steep hill. Snowshoers, hikers, and bikers are expected to stay off groomed ski trails.

Single Track Mountain Bike Trails
(see map on page 9)

About 15 miles of single track trails exist in the park. They vary in difficulty from moderate to difficult. At trail intersections, trail signs indicate your location and trail difficulty ahead. Snowshoeing, summer/winter hiking, and biking are permissible on single track bike trails.

Park Animals

Mammals

Most park visitors rarely see many park mammals as they are rather secretive and move around mostly at dusk or at night. By hiking quietly, you are more likely to encounter some of the larger mammals. The most common mammals include deer, coyotes, red and gray foxes, flying squirrels, chipmunks, thirteen-lined ground squirrels, woodchucks, raccoons, cottontail rabbits, opossums, weasels, and skunks. Smaller mammals include meadow, deer, jumping, house, and harvest mice; prairie moles; and two kinds of shrews.

Birds

Between the spring and fall migrants and resident nesting birds, one might see as many as 150 birds in a single year in the park. Of the resident nesting birds (about 75 species), the following are the most common: wild turkeys; turkey vultures; red-tailed and Cooper's hawks; scarlet tanagers; Baltimore orioles; rose-breasted grosbeaks; wood pewees; crested and least flycatchers; blue jays; crows; great horned, barred, and screech owls; red-headed, red-bellied, hairy, downy, and pileated woodpeckers; ruffed grouse; house wrens; chickadees; bluebirds; indigo buntings; towhees; catbirds; chestnut-sided warblers; red-starts; red-winged blackbirds; red-eyed and warbling vireos; robins; song, vesper and chipping sparrows. About fifteen bird species are year-round residents. Those species along with about another dozen species make up those that can be seen during the winter.

Notes

Notes

Notes

Notes

Notes

Notes

Notes

Printed in the United States
by Baker & Taylor Publisher Services